Dear Eddie, even as you go uphill
in our history, you take reconstruction
seriously and with enthusiasm. I wish
you much luck.
Noah.

Echoes of a past world

Noah K. Ndosi

Mzumbe Book Project,
P.O. Box 113,
Mzumbe - Morogoro.

First Published 1993

Printed & bound by
Mzumbe Book Project

Contents

To Dr. Moses N. Ndosi

And now,
reflections of that light
you cast along your path
have with years ripened:
the impulses from within
are difficult to contain

In those early days,
acquisition of education
was such an exacting ordeal
but now,
after years of protractions
success sparks joy

Though only in glimpses,
these poems
are in part a mirror
of that challenging past
we trode through.

Noah K. Ndosi

Echoes of a Past World

Where are the times,
when the distant horizon
was the end of the world
we so well knew,
a world, firmly protected
by the strength of the spear?

When we trapped antelopes
as our herds multiplied,
filling expanded kraals,
when warriors retired with bulls
in to the thickness of woods
to nurse strong blood?

Tell me,
where are those times,
when warriors growled
to reassure peace
amidst roaming lions?

When people met at night
and celebrated in felt
ancestral rhythms,
when the world was but
a ball under the mighty sun?

The times,
when old men discussed
weighty issues in a single day
and wove riddles
to harness the wisdom of life?

When disease found cure
in concoction of herbs,
and death moaned truthfully,
the time? when
a man chewed snuff

and spat confidently
without fear of being
tipped over.

Yes,
tell me,
where are the times,
the time when ....

In the Evening

In the evening
when cows are home,
I walk past trees,
fluffy, fluffy
whispers the air;
cares of a busy world
begin to fade away
glimpses of a promising
night linger on.

In the evening,
when I return home
from tedious labouring
In the fields,
I drink hot soup
and enjoy juicy meat;
tiredness melts away
from the bones
and thirst fades off;
from the silence
of dark bushes,
worms begin to glow:
life unmasks its face.

In the evening,
when the tumult
of a celebration
is peacefully wound up,
children sit attentively
as elder turns take
narrating stories of old:
hearts are renewed
as the old past
and future starts
to brighten with hope.

The Smell of Death

Our neighbour ill,
words filter through
in quiet murmurs

Early morning
as the first cock crows,
men throw blankets
to one side
and tip-toe to the ill

In a dark apartment
under heavy cover,
a severely emaciated
body is immersed
in attacks of violent coughs
which culminated in bloody mucus

Experts go for roots,
odd mixtures are taken,
rams are slaughtered,
rituals are performed
at the ancestors graves,
but no ray of hope.

People retire home silently
for they have done
the best they knew:
a shower of rain falls,
gloom pervades the neighbourhood
death hangs low.

Another Grazing Day

Without a streak of cloud,
the sun puts on a face of
blinding intensity;
the earth gapes with cracks
while layers of dust
like carpets cover paths

Under the big umbrella-tree,
a flock of sheep and goats
in a pool of shade
chew repeatedly in silence;
tiny flies invade the air
while loneliness pricks
like an unseen thorn

A gentle rustle
steal away
on an ant-hill,
coloured lizards
vigorously chase
one another
while a coiled serpent
on a twig flashes
a forked tongue
like dancing flames

As if by magic,
a whirlwind starts spinning:
blown awake, the herd
nibbles here and there;
my foggy mind ruffled up,
I yawn widely:
an old song reenters memory,
I sing to tiredness.

My Dwindling Goats

My healthy goat
which just delivered
is seized by strange powers

After mounts of pain,
it delivered a graceful baby
like new moon

But when the mother
smells the baby,
she snorts disapprovingly,
she tosses the kid
out of reach

My big, fat he-goat
triggered envy
as his domineering presence
lead the herd
but the other day,
he was found stiff and cold
his bowels as big
as pumpkins:
we buried him whole,
deep, down a pit

A leopard broke into my kraal:
he walked off with a fat one;
the jaws of a straying dog
snapped on a tender leg
of a frightened kid:
it died of the wound

I have done
no man wrong,
but even madness
has dared an arrow
against my dwindling goats!

Taking My Love to Town

Christmas near again my love,
I shall take you down town,
present you
to the best of tailors;
he will measure you
as your eye pleases
even if costs amount
to whole cow,
mind not

On Christmas day,
eyes will burn with curiosity
feeding on your details:
as you walk in
and out of church,
you will be a blooming star;
your own grandmother
will not recognize you
from a distance

In a well tided neighbourhood,
you will be a special guest
of uplifted honour
as you feed on delicious meals
and refreshing drinks

The uncountable days
of an ugly past
will be suspended;
throughout the festivity
my love,
you will be the brightest star
in the best tides of time.

In those Days

In those thrilling days
of childhood,
my daily task
was to tend
a handful of goats,
I wriggled and dashed about
like quicksilver

I called each by name:
hairs ruffled,
ears up lifted,
it came to me
and licked my palms

I listened to snakes,
smelled poisonous grass
and ploughed through
knee-reaching mud
without streaks of fear;
to confirm the success
of the day,
I simply observed
the distended bowels
of the animals

I would look
at the sky
and simply remark:
"today, it will rain"
it rained

I rode fat oxen
like a chief
and smelled my way
through darkness;
when I smiled at the moon,
it smiled back

I had the names of game
on my fingertips,
I knew singing birds,
buzzing insects;
happy and contented,
I walked hand in hand
with embracing nature.

Mayaa Nkuu

A bamboo-pole
on shoulders
of young, strong men,
a body sags in between
tied by ropes
as solemn feet
tread to the grave-yard

Heaving with grief,
a daughter weeps bitterly:
attempts to console her abort
men stare on helplessly
as vanity ascertains itself

Her warm hut empty,
her gourds,
her best necklace
hanging on a rack
-all without an owner,
even her cows got wind of it:
they moo into the depths
of a silent night

With wrinkled faces
people file the path,
the day's story
is patched up,
the gossip is passed on:
Mayaa NKUU,
the oldest of roots
in the village
had retired to bed
the night before,
the following morning,
she was picked up
cold and stiff.

Warm Assurance

She is an old girl,
whose salty tears
after much longing
and quiet waiting
have wetted patience

By the village-paths
the gossip is cn
as mothers,
like industrious beavers
split the topic
enjoying the fine threads
of enchanting details

Taking delight
in elevated jokes,
men clear their throats:
they sip in calabashes of brew
life bursting with
reassuring colours

Though long lost
in a vale of despair,
meanness has óf late
found seat high up
in the sky of hope
for an old village maid
is in glowing favours
of a lover's assurance.

Death of an Agemate

At night,
news of a friend's death
reached a family:
clouds spread over hearts:
people wondered
at the illness
which crept unseen
to devour the strength
of a well known man

As the early sun
gently dismissed pockets
of remaining darkness,
a man walked
a rod in hand,
supporting himself
to a brewing shed
to soothe the hard
blow of death

The deceased was recalled:
how lively had he played
with several agemates?
The initiations they had
ritually undergone,
how industriously
had they laboured
at their inlaws,
as they proposed to marry?

They had slaughtered
fat rams and goats
when their wives
were blessed with children;
had they not pinched snuff
from one anothers' palms and happily drank

from the same calabashes
hugging one another?
How had life been
but a majestic mid-day sun?

Seated in dark chambers,
a widow was all but tears;
receiving condolence,
she once again wetted
the cruel links of time

And the little ones,
how uncomprehendingly
they stared on?
Had father only left
for a temporary sleep?
How would they make it
without his warm guidance?

A bull was slaughtered,
meat was passed round,
calabashes moved
from mouth to mouth,
shadows lengthened
and the day aged;
grief was sealed
in past stores of time
as people retired home,
quietness posed over
intensifying the mourning.

The Rain that Fell

The rain that fell
began with soft drizzling
and a colourful rainbow
which danced in the horizon;
darkness intervened
the rains poured down
as if the heavens
were at war

Lightning and thunder
sparked and spelled danger:
an old tree
was knocked down
Hmmm!
The path has a new bend

Caught unprepared in the plains,
we were soaked to the skin:
clothes stuck tightly
to our shivering cold bodies
we paced about restlessly
like wet chickens

A hut that had bravely stood
by the cow-path
lay on its belly;
cursing his ill-luck,
the owner busied himself
looking for a supporting post

The heavy rain that fell
was bloated away
by the scorching sun
but it will surely
fall again
to catch people on journey
quite unaware again.

The **Dance**

Waists girded,
arms on shoulders,
chatters float about
as young men and women
make a wide ring
in where a leader stands

A woman's soft voice
bursts forth:
after hesitations,
a chorus is on the swing:
once,twice, and
the dance is on

Round after round,
forward and backward,
breasts rise and fall,
sweat trickles down
and the earth drinks fast.

From a distance,
old folks stare
with mounting curiosity;
an old lady forgets herself:
ear-rings dangle:
backwards and forward,
up and down:
she is youthful
jerks and swings

The cock,
the dog
and children,
all stand absorbed
as the air picks up
intoxicating rhythm,
dust rising gently.

Death

From our cemetery,
a tone is dripping:
soft and sorrowful,
its message
paralyzes the world:
one has left us again

In the near farms,
some stop working;
they walk about
whispering for details
while others gather up
and retreat home
full of fear

The bell is tolling:
silence hangs
over the land;
hearts are stung
with an unfading message
for death is strong
and everlasting

The bell is tolling;
mourning soaks hearts;
life is diluted
to a transient dream;
weeks roll by
wounds heal slowly,
hearts unfold again
and sweet life
swells to normal.

Kun! Kun!........

Gathered in ancient rags,
a firm grip on a shaky rod,
even the path teases him:
Kun! Kun!............

He reaches a deep furrow:
fear mounts on him;
immersed in a pool of doubts,
he summons his dim vision
and strides across
in a chain of hesitations
like a dry branch of a tree
at the mercy of the wind

Wrapped in a blanket
of worrisome frailty,
decrepit age negotiates
for a stroll along the ways:
kun! kun!.........

Kuu, Kukuru! Kuru ku!.

The new moon retired
past midnight,
children snored audibly
as echoes of melancholy
pierced interlocking canopy:
Uuu, Kukuru! Kuru, ku!........

After countless days
of painful moaning,
the headman's wife
in a forlorn night,
lay in difficult moments
awaiting to embark
on a journey
from which no one returns

After the second cock-crow,
the sun struggled upward
filtering its young rays
from down below;
sighs of moaning
awakened the slumbering world

Silently and solemnly,
men and women converged:
detail of how and why
were curiously woven:
the sooth-sayer's words
sank with prophetic validity
as triumphant death descended

Tum! Tom! Tim! Tam!....

It is many hours
since nightly silence
over the village descended:
Tum! Tom! Tim! Tam!..........

For quite sometime,
rhythm like trotting hooves
spills over the village
from across a valley:
Tam! Tom! Tim! Tum!..........

These neighbourhoods
are poverty-striken
and the spark of celebration
is a seldom one:
Tom! Tum! Tam! Tim!..........

Waves of speculations
float about:
perhaps a celebration
of ancestors,
some marriage-feast,
perhaps pressing nostalgia:
Tim! Tom! Tam! Tum!..........

Temptations of joining
the excitement rise
like a high tide
but, Kwa Bulaanga
are strange neighbourhoods,
those who dare in at night
hardly return:
Tum! Tom! Tim! Tam!..........

21

The Land is Ours

The sun creeping overhead,
one after another,
they arrive under Nringaringa,
a towering umbrella-tree,
their usual meeting place

The headman,
in a serious tone
spells out the issue
of the day,
speakers, in quick series
warm up the core of the case,
the issue, so vividly perceived
like an outstretched cowhide;
how dare they
loosen their hands?
What will they tell
children and wives?
Will later generations
ever pardon them?

The sun dances overhead
then takes to the West;
a sense of firmness ripens,
jaws tighten up;
a resolution is born:
"Come what may,
the land is ours!
God is on our side,
Aaaamen!"

Throats dry,
the weight of the day
settled down,
the meeting comes to an end;
bowels churn with hunger,
they leave for the brew
for they must gather strength
for the worst possible!

Do not Despise

Do not despise:
big rolling eyes
in deep crators
of a big, skinny head,
weak, bulby knees
slung on a mother's back,
- a wailing lump
on the margins of life

Days will unfold,
the sap of life
will return;
clutching a spear
and a shield,
he will ward off
intruders in the land

His blood ripe,
life will rise higher,
after paying a chain
of cows and rams,
he will take a wife
and begin to multiply
his own like

Counting the produce
from his folds,
he will sit back,
converse judiciously
with fleeting time;
old age will gently
invade him;
his days dimmer,
he will retire to the ground
like an old banana-stem
letting new blood shoot up.

A Broken Heart

~Their marriage still young,
life assumed a kink suddenly:
a mysterious illness
slowly killed her husband

Years rolled away,
time splashed its anger
inflicting deep stabs
of loneliness on her:
in drowning waves
of doubts and despondency,
she called on the Almighty
in her silent heart,
her prayer book, ever close

From deep pools
of great strength,
she stood firmly
looking after her herds
of sheep and goats;
she toiled all seasons
reaping bounteous crops
while raising up her children
with untiring determination

Broken down by mighty time,
sometimes, she is all tears,
she walks on, eyes uplifted
to the silent, dark heavens,
hoping firmly that providence
will soothen her deep aches.

The Mad Man

Dressed in bundles
of patchy, hanging clothes,
the mad man is a stranger
from far away

When his madness is at peaks,
he sings himself hoarse
and makes jumpy dances
which fall in rhythm
with spurts of his whistle

He appeared at the market-place:
he drew people like a magnet,
as he cut the air
with dancing jerks,
he sweated and his rags
flew in the wind:
he was garlanded the hero
of the day

Without a house
or a family,
he sleeps where
a nightly mat unfolds

He disappeared
for some time:
he was taken for lost
or even dead

But the other day,
he emerged at a road-junction:
entertaining crowds,
they offered him
ripe bananas and
pinches of snuff

He talks to himself
mumbling strange stuff:
people say,
his head is different:
it runs like fast water!

The lorry

The dry season ripe,
maize-harvesting is on;
the road up the hills
is a blanket of dust

As it climbs up-hill,
the lorry screams with pains
of felt overloadedness:
it rolls slowly; upwardly
ejecting massive clouds
of intoxicating smoke

The distant roaring
like a powerful magnet
attracts chattering children,
who by the road-side applaud:
"Fire! Give it fire!"

The driver wipes his brow,
the bush vibrates.
the high sun trembles
and a squirrel takes chance
frantically dashing
across the difficult road

A heap of faggots
on her aching head,
the lorry catches up
with a weary woman,
who gives way with a sigh,
wondering at the mysteries
of man-made, rattling monsters

At long last,
the road reaches a curve:
the driver engages

with acrobatic skills
round, dark knobs,
amidst jerks and jolts:
the lorry responds
with an even tone
as it slithes farther on

The Murderer

Alcohol flowed
in the village,
moods warmed up,
forgotten wounds
were easily bruised

Anger flared up:
clubs trembled
in nervous hands;
as two men faced each other,
terror gripped the air

Men drank off
the last offers
of a bride-price;
a young man
hit a neighbour
with a wild log:
the drunk man collapsed
a fountain of blood oozing;
after three days
his stars gave up,
he curled up dead

The young man
was whisked into prison;
years sped by,
the village forgot him;
an amnesty was declared:
he returned home
only to sink deeper
in a barrel of alcohol

Strange powers seized him:
at night, he wandered off
into mysterious wilderness;

after weeks,
he took off surreptitiously
to distant lands;
his worried family
became a flock without a herder

Relatives raked the plains
without a distant trace
of his marks;
on the verge of dispair,
at the bottom of a crator,
his poor, tired body
was found soaked
in a heap of decaying stench:
even hyenas did not touch him.

A Black Serpent

The three-o'clock sun aflame,
the world, worn out
by exhaustive toiling,
thoughts stray loosely
along a circuitous path

A few steps ahead,
a black serpent
flows swiftly
across the narrow path;
on a stony mound,
it raises its hood
displaying annoyance
in sharp, dotty eyes
and a forked tongue
dancing like flames

The girl freezes with fright,
arm-pits dripping sweat,
her heart pounding wildly,
she hurredly beats
stretches of windy paths,
eventually reaching the farm

Assailed by currents
of suspicion, she industriously
weeds a flowering crop of beans,
cuts a heavy bundle of grass
and trots back home,
full of the day's encounter

After an evening meal
protection hugging them,
she picks up courage
unfolding the details
of her encounter

by the fireside;
swallowing details
in great appetite,
sleep rubs on their eyes
each retiring to bed
in currents of excitement.

The Village Headman

He was a simple
widow's son,
who thrived and excelled
amidst corrugations of life:
he become a famous warrior

Cries of war
echoed over the land:
a sparkling spear
in his right hand,
he fought with such courage,
he returned a hero
received at the village-entrance

When severe drought
threatened the land,
he spearheaded digging
a long canal,
blisters bursting
with stinging pains;
sappy life restored,
children smiled full of hope

Inescapable time
caught up with him:
his face wrinkled with age,
his hair scanty and ashy,
his hands stiff knuckles,
he sat in tranquillity
narrating from stores
which escorted young minds
to bottomless depths

Aches of Desperation

Engaging a strong tongue,
she treads behind
a handful of goats
which dash wildly
outwitting her poor vision

The scorching sun merciless,
worries, like rising tides
drifted through her mind:
the burial of an industrious husband
and her two children at a tender age,
the death of her cow
while delivering a fat calf,
and repeated failure of her crops,
only God knew her losses

Her stooping frame
full of sorts of pains,
her stomach hardening
without appetite,
even her once composed soul
has become vulnerable
to trivial bruises
for bursts of tears
alternate with laughter,
loneliness having triumphed
over her.

War-Front Hero

Once again
old Mang'ile falters
with drunkenness
of an aging day;
he cocks himself up
and spurs the village
to peaks of excitement

He burns forth
with breath-taking tales
from far off,
across the seas, inwhere,
he spent gruelling months
fighting strange people

The details of war
shaky to his rusty memory,
fascinated by survival
through countless knots
and of course
his K.A.R-uniforms,
he is a bright star

In an open area,
infront of his compound,
he stiffens up with demonstrations
of slow marches,
arms ready,
salute and fire!

Stimulated by their own,
his wives and children
absorb him with renewed admiration
for his present world
is a mere spark:
old Mang'ile,
our war-front hero.

Poor Old Man

Nursing jiggered toes
in sweaty, old rags,
he sits on a bare stone
as the burning sun
pours its anger on him

Bitterness simmers within
as thick fingers fumble
in depths of ancient folds
teeming with blood-thirsty bugs

A few leaps away,
a flock of sheep and goats
in a pool of shade
converge heads in a scrum;
the browsing fields arid,
the animals panting
like hounds, then,
after fruitless hours
of expansive grazing
hunger presses them

Caught in a bizarre stare,
stubborn life has crushed him
back into helpless childhood:
a whirl-wind spins up dust
and dumps it on him:
he sneezes and curses

Despite the pricking mockery,
he swallows the thorns of life
vowing to defend his bits
of scattered possessions
till restless time
would maul him off
this shameless world!

The Man who Lay Ill

The man,
who for years lay ill,
unaware of his whereabouts
and muttering nonsense,
is on the path again

Like a prisoner
released after a long sentence,
he is curiously studying
his surroundings again:
weak and light on the path,
he is overcautious

People shake warm hands,
welcoming him back,
they sigh with relief
for he had severally
been on dangerous peaks:
hope scattered away,
eyes had swollen up
any time to mourn death

As he walks around,
a newness greets his eyes;
having survived narrowly,
he is a new being
thirsty of life
driven by rays
of hope within.

Neekuywa

It is an old lady
whose rags weigh
heavily on her
shrunken bones:
they are so old,
millet would do well
on those layers

But today,
as she walks down
the village-path,
history is reversed;
pin-point aware
as she avoids
touching shrubs,
she walks in uplifted trotting:
indeed,
she is a new leaf

Those who best know her
disbelieve their eyes;
full of excitement,
they elevate her:
"how beautiful!
Who was the tailor?
Turn round and walk on!
Neekuywa mama,
it is not your true self!
You are a borrowed one!"

Broken Heart

He walks in hesitations
stopping in some shade,
wherein he is immersed
in disturbing thoughts

Dizziness drifts across
his failing memory
for his heart is heavy:
he would have forgotten all,
but................

It is a village man
whose wife delivered
a precious baby:
a baby named after
a grand ancestor;
he had gathered his purse
and hit the roads to town
insearch of a fat ram

From far away,
pick-pockets spotted him
as he clumsily
moved about slowly,
the cleverness of town
too intricate for him

Enjoying his unguarded moves,
they secretly smiled
at their chances of success;
he reached a fascinating shop
and studied various prices of inviting goods;
his thin neck up
like a dazzled giraffe,
surreptitiously, a cruel arm
scooped off a bundle of notes:
his only savings

41

A weak, hungry wife
who had just delivered,
a grandmother and
a neighbourhood
expecting some nourishing soup
and delicious roasting ....
Staggering on,
he stared into hazy
distant horizons,
approaching an expectant home
emptiness ascertained itself
with crushing solidity:
How he would have clubbed
the thieving devil
to bleeding death, but ....

The Man who Walks About

The man
who walks about
left on a distant journey:
the neighbourhood is quiet

Without the warmth
of a mother,
without the guidance
of a father,
he grew up singly
like a maize-stalk
in the wilderness

Before people leave
for their farms
to toil in there,
he roams in and out
of several homes
avidly enjoying
heaps of bananas,
sour meals and leftovers

A skinny goat died somewhere,
the owner abandoned it
for his starved dogs
but the man appeared soon:
outwitting children with tales,
he dragged the goat
in secret bushes,
roasting it with delight,
he filled his stomach
like a tight drum:
nothing harms him!

The other day,
a mysterious illness
gripped him:
before the village
took note of it,
he suddenly collapsed:
all is quiet.

The Cursed

Born healthy,
he grew up
herding cattle;
    a big boy
of admirable strength

Ill-luck blew his way:
the devil lured him;
he stole to a beehive
and harvested honey
to silence his hunger

Months transpired:
a curse stuck on him,
from loose jaws
saliva dripped down;
he reeled swayingly
as if he would tumble next
and his hands danced
shaky tremors
no one understood

I accidentally annoyed him:
eyes wide open,
he welled up with rage:
mumbling spurts of abuses,
he shook and trembled
as if a monster
had seized him

When the villagers meet him,
they greet him,
they let him pass;
full of perplexity,
they ponder the depths
of his curse.

Worries over Son

Far away,
the silent mountain
peaks to the blue heavens;
across stretches
of grazing plains,
a man trots behind
a handful of sheep
and skinny goats,
a dexterous eye
straining to lead them
where lush grass thrives

The mighty sun
pours down in great strength;
his memory burning
like a silent flame,
he ponders the disappearance
of his son in solitudes

A message of death
of an unknown labourer
from a distant estate
filters through:
his face, rows of wrinkles
drowned in worries,
he is unable to sleep;
lighning had pierced
through his heart severally,
the end of the world
seeming quite near

And the neighbour
with whom he converses
into depths of nights
has a ripe daughter:
had he married off

his son earlier,
might he, at least, not
have drawn consolation
from a grandchild?

A goat rushes
into a thriving crop:
running and cursing,
creepers entangle him;
he falls down
like a little child
but rises in good time
to avert a greedy mouth
off the delicate crop

At last, the day pities him;
the sun hides behind trees,
shadows lengthen,
his head dizzy,
he takes comfort in winding
up another day
as he leads the beasts home.

Mama Somi

When morning breaks,
she closes her hut,
picks up her old tools,
departs to farm

Swaying a stumpy hoe,
she wears herself
to dizzy tiredness;
she takes sips of rest
recalling those days
when her children
had noisily played
around the hearth,
the lively celebrations
she had intensely enjoyed,
how brightly had the sun
shone on her paths!

A dear husband,
mysteriously dead,
her daughters married off
to strangers:
it is the bleating sheep
which keeps her company

When she cooks a meal,
she loses her appetite,
it is the neighbour's children
who finish it up;
once in an enviable hut,
it now reels with cracks
of age
and figures well
in the jokes of the village

The death of a neighbour
floats about:
she descends into a pool
of deep ruminations;
she murmurs to herself:
"The world is old,
I shall retire to bed
some night,
the following morning,
I shall be gone
like the wind
to join the ancestors."

Hunting

Our hunting grounds
clusters of thorny shrubs,
they richly harboured
sorts of wild game;
starting from the entrance
of our village,
they spread outwardly
into the fading horizons

On an agreed day,
spears, matchets and clubs
were brandished high;
a stone was flung
into pockets of thickets:
a fat buck sprang
into the open;
an army of dogs
backed deafeningly sharp
as they flew after the prey

Excitement opened
an untrodden chapter:
surrounded by danger
from all sides,
the buck flew frantically:
it rolled down
steep, rocky cliffs

The animal landed in a pool
of a splashing thud, on stones:
it fragmented to pieces
and blood sputtered about;
hurredly heaving with excitement,
the hunters sought a quick path
down the river-bottom;
as if teasing them,

the river washed down
the meat amidst hesitations

Mouths watering,
hounds growled
as the hunters watched
the loss of a rich harvest
in a pool of helplessness;
cursing their ill-luck,
they returned disappointed
the river flowing thunderously.

Our Neighbours

When the new moon
was sighted,
men wore long robes,
women dressed in
colourful kangas
like butterflies

Down and up the roads,
they sang and danced
in youthful tides;
the crushing ordeals
of a life-time labourer
evaporated for a while
life assuming new heights

Amidst marimba-rhythms,
bodies wriggled and swayed
across expanses of plains
Ululululu..................
Dust rose high

But today,
silence, like dew
poses over the settlement;
whispers and murmurs
float about

The oldest man,
popular Baba Juma,
who wove exciting stories
from his dusty and
kinky life
-a well respected elderly
has died mysteriously

Neighbours gathered
in mournful tones
they celebrated the uncertainty
of maverick life:
women shed painful tears,
like a rain going through
a dilapidated roof,
loneliness overpowers
the settlement again.

Kasava

After two brothers
and a sister were born,
he suffered waves of neglect:
hunger scorched him more,
but when food, by luck,
was eventually available,
it was tasteless banana-meals
that turned away even dogs

His stomach swelled up:
mothers claimed that
he harboured a pot of worms
his toes thick and weeping,
they hid fat jiggers,
an irritating yellow slime
ran down his nose

He sometimes dashed
after a restless goat:
feet twisted sideways,
the wind blew his rags
to one side
exposing a big tummy
flying on thin sticks;
we held our breasts
as rasps of laughter
echoed across

He often stumbled
and fell down;
he curled up and wept
with tearful pains;
leading our herds home,
he was feverish,

limbs full of sores,
beyond all doubts
his existence was
a hard negotiation
on naked rocks.

Grandma Unfolds Again

The day bright,
the sun trembles:
the call for water,
quite a frequent one

In sweet silence
of our neighbourhood,
grandma sits in a shade
meditating alone
in tight embraces
of grey age

Tired after much play,
our restlessness
poked into her vague
stores of memory:
like ashy ambers,
she stirred up
full of her past

Captured in a war,
she had trotted
by her motherside
as victorious warriors
escorted a big herd
of cattle home

In a strange land,
she had industriously
fought wilderness,
claiming new land;
her rams fat,
her cows full of milk,
the village had carried her praises over shoulder
for like a weed,
she had thrived on doubtful soils

Looking at herself,
she felt her folds of thin skin;
weak and unsure along the paths,
she sighed and called herself
a useless tuft.

When Isambu Goes Down

When Isambu goes down,
strides agile and steady,
his tartered rags
flying in the wind,
his throat then dry,
life will be calm
añd sober

With the coming back
of the evening cattle-herd,
he will be heard singing
far down the valley:
"I live on my sweat, haa!
I was circumcised
in daylight, hoo!
I was legally married,
haa hoi!"

The village path
will noisily fill up
with little children
who, delightedly turn up
enjoying and teasing him

His throat soaked,
the world in colours,
tunes of life
will vibrated in him
as he moves on staggering
into his night shelter.

There Walks a Woman

There walks a woman,
an ancient plank of beehive
above a twisted neck,
she carries neatly
rowed bananas
in collected strength
to win a shilling
for a gourd of milk

Though feeble,
she cocks herself
in hard determination,
the message floating
on her head clearly:
"Banana! Banana ripe!
Stranger, see! Cheap!
Banana buy!"

. The sky opens up
pouring down severe heat
into the passive earth;
she spends the whole day
at one side
of a main road:
"Banana! Banana, ripe!
Stranger, see!
Banana buy, cheap!"

Like a valiant fighter
on a special mission,
she defends loose bowels
of her only son
whose health is dwindling.

The Stranger and our Land

A stranger
came to our land;
he knew well
how to tame ferocity
to achieve an aim

He called the chief aside;
amidst soft murmurs,
he thickly smeared him
with fabricated praises
which puffed him up

My mother had laboriously
broken down her land:
she had retired home
to fetch her assorted seeds

When she returned,
the stranger was busy
laying a foundation
of a big house;
a gun on shoulder,
he barked: "Go away!"
His hounds lifted it higher

His greedy eye
ate the land,
barbed wire
followed behind,
the land,
land of the people contracted!

The case was documented
in special files,
files of bias for the stranger:
procrastinations, a game
of tactics without end

People's anger grew
against the chief;
how could they stomach
daylight robbery of justice?
A sage summed it up
in knotty bitterness:
"May heaven burst
his entrails!"

Oho,
The chief wrinkled with pains,
his stomach swelled,
death nodded timely!

Old Men

And old men talk,
talk endlessly,
meat, they chew,
chew repeatedly:
softness so agreeable
to broken age

Brave yesterday,
young, strong blood
darted fast
into thickest of thickets
in impevious darkness;
leopards and lions
were speared to death

Today,
the past delights
in tons of mockery,
cries of danger
alarm the village,
women, children and
tremulous old men
in blankets of frailty,
all rush for door-entrances
into dark chambers
with hearts flying
against their ribs.

Victim of Hunger

His hut on hilly ground,
people walking by
recognized him:
a slim, tall man
on whose narrow face
peaceful eyes rested;
slow and of few words,
he always walked alone
up and down the ways

A new season came:
the defiant sun rose,
stubbornly refusing
to hide its face;
greenness was devoured
as the world shrank
into brown tufts
and clouds of thick dust

He slipped into gaping jaws
of ruthless time:
pangs of hunger
scorched him,
although he sought refuge
at his sister's,
death beckoned at him
and he responded
in consuming weakness

Although many years
have sped by,
mystery haunts
his forlorn compound
as if to question
his untimely death.

Ikurubu

Danger pierces the night,
children and women tremble;
with spears and matchets,
men summon up courage
fortifying their bounds
as they head on
to the grounds of danger

But Ikurubu,
a well known exception
will sternly warn his family
not to betray his whereabouts

Once called by a woman
to kill a small snake,
he wildly beat the bush
boasting to have put on
the best of fights

In a dark evening,
shrieks of a wild cat
set his voice trembling;
when thunder rumbled,
a lump of chewing tobacco
slipped down his throat:
women laugh at him,
they say he wears the heart
of a woman

But when celebrations
tickle the neighbourhood,
his voice above others,
he flavours details
sparking vibrant laughter:
they say his stories
would set hyenas giggling.

Such is a Woman

Early morning
while the sun's beauty
is veiled in envious clouds,
a mother's mind
burns with concern

A curved knife
in one hand,
banana-fibres
in the other,
her feet are agile
tip-toeing into bushes
while ashen grass
drips with morning dew

Engaging dexterous hands,
she mows tufts of grass,
she rakes the wilderness
with little success
till she reaches a riverside,
where she is lastly rewarded

A bundle of heavy grass
on her spine,
she staggers home
hands and feet numb,
while people marvel
at her sense of duty

She feeds her children,
cleans her house,
feeds the animals,
and departs to farm
where, she bends her back
till sun-set.

Men passing by recall her mother
and marvel at how life
reproduces like,
quietly approving,
"such is a woman".

My Aunt

Who knows
what young age
will ripen to?
She has diligently
watch_d the growth
of a nephew

At farm,
she always instructed us
how best to deal
with a hoe
-a pen with which
to defend life

Exhausted,
we frequently lost interest;
she spured us on
emphasizing repeatedly
that blisters averted hunger!

When I had fever,
mornings and evenings,
she turned up
summoning me to
tighten my belt:
for though difficulties
tasted nasty,
they made one grow

In high school,
she kept sharp scrutiny
on my trivial engagements,
always intergrating
school learning
into the village-world

But it is the clarity
of conscience
and her strong judicious mind
that cast most light
on her life:
when a neighbour delivered,
she abandoned her farms
serving the young mother,
her door-entrance teems
with people seeking reconciliations;
settling a family problem,
she shares her only pinch
of snuff with a neighbour

Her children grown up,
age having gripped
the upper hand,
after all that life
has taught her,
she entertains an unwavering
conviction:
even with best efforts,
all achievement is the
Almighty's own granting!

At Farm in July

A spider is busy
spinning a play-field
of glassy, fine network;
the wind distills
waves of rustling,
the bumble bee dances
from tops of blooming
dark-green cowpeas;
in frantic leaps,
a duicker scampers off
near green shrubs;
a twittering bird
singularly applauds
the promising yield;
peace walks into mind
as dew trickles down
with hesitations
to mother earth;
then, cool July
is on the march again.

Reaping at the Edge of Hope

That particular year
began just like others;
hands were light
timely preparing the farms
for planting

The sun persistently angry,
dust thickened
and the streams
that had overflown
during the rains
dried up

At night,
dreams were of rains,
by day,
eyes raked the heavens,
but in vain;
the stubborn sun
danced on above

Solid hope found
thin dilution,
desperation took root:
people tightened belts
as hunger began
to frighten people

Out of no where,
the sky frowned;
thunder exploded
like deafening bombs:
heavy pours followed

Children were quick
taking delight,
peeling off clothes,
they dashed for hail-stones
playing and rejoicing
at the -blessing of rain

Every farmer
responded timely:
planting extensively
and weeding cautiously,
at the very edge of despair,
they harvested as heavily
as they had seldom chanced.

Murder

An evening ripened,
echoes of shouts
from men celebrating
a dowry of local brew
were now soft murmurs
of a fading event

Out of the unseen,
a quarrel flared up:
a man chased another,
at a door-entrance,
a club descended
on the head of one:
oozing blood,
he crumbled down
like a defenseless lump

In her watchful curiosity,
grandmother had followed
the chase from a distance:
stormed by grunts of
a dying person at her entrance,
she shouted for help
protesting against murder
at her door-entrance

People flocked in:
a bowl of milk
at the mouth of the wounded
turned bloody
and was discarded:
news spread fast,
fear increased
with darkness

The wounded struggled
in a deep sea of
loneliness and agony;
three days,
his stars dimmed:
death triumphed

Years are now gone,
but as feet traverse
the neighbourhood,
an emptiness lingers on
for the home
that was once solidly fortified
is a reed in merciless currents.

The Pawpaw Tree

Short and sappy
it stood firmly
by the village path
bearing fruits
larger than a man's head

Our stomachs churning
with hunger once,
we harvested a ripe pawpaw;
sweet and fleshy,
it quenched thirst:
our bellies swelled up

After several seasons,
it acquired a long, thin neck,
a stumpy head
with fist-sized fruits

People remarked that
like an old cow,
the pawpaw-tree was giving in
to the weight of time

The other day,
a storm whisked about;
the pawpaw tree
lost its head,
like a post,
it stands bare
and forsaken.

A Bitter Tongue

Full of bitter complaints,
she wakes up early
drowning the early singing bird
with a fiery tongue

Her world was once calm and orderly;
of late,
her children
have grown horns
against her

One is a known thief,
another has turned
into a fighting bull
and her daughter,
her only hope,
has grown a stiff neck:
she acts as she pleases

They rebel against her:
insulting her,
they threaten to strangle her
calling her a snake
with a long tongue

Before the day begins,
people make for her entrance:
they pile claims of stolen property,
and of their wounded sons:
they call her a witch!
A noxious weed in the village!

Driven to peaks of anger,
she burts forth:
"Why did I end up
with such children,
such filthy dogs?

They scramble for sweet things
but shun work!
May they vanish! Yes,
may they all end up
in the deep valley
in the fast currents
of the angry river,
where no one returns!"

The Summon

Dancing tassels
on a red tarboosh,
the court-guard
appeared suddenly
as an old man
absorbed curiously
the browsing
of his cows

Stormed by a long letter
which he did not understand,
he sighed apprehensively
swearing loudly by God
not to have touched
anyone's property

He vehemently cursed
a stubborn world
which had lost respect
for word of mouth;
he wandered off
as the night intensified
to an agemete
whose son was in the highest
ladder of learning

At last, the letter,
like a riddle was interpreted:
several months previously
at a nearby celebration,
a man had been wounded,
despite a long treatment
in a reputed hospital,
the man had died:
witnesses were then summoned!

The night heavy
like a grinding stone
on his chest,
he was fascinated by
the lightheadedness
of the new age;
his memory thick for details,
he cursed an arrogant world
so bookish that it would not
let bygones be gone!
Could they call back life?

As the cock crew,
before eyes could outline paths,
he was up hills
trotting across rivers;
they say,
he was the first
to appear in court.

A Crowning Grazing Day

Bowels hanging loosely,
hooves knocking,
joints cracking nuts,
tails uplifted,
warm droppings splashing,
some sour smell rising,
a cattle herd
reels down a dusty cow-path

Like confluent rivers,
two herds meet:
the beasts smell each other
as if to establish
a broken kinship;
moos echo across
the vastness of plains

Two bulls stand eye to eye:
they sniffle and snort
in despicable reproach;
within twinkles,
horns interlock:
the probe of strength
becomes an exciting drama

After exhaustion
from repeated wrangles,
the weaker bull   ·
in quick, reverse trots
is thrust into a pool;
of dark, sharp thorns
inwhere, it groans
fully contained in humiliation

The winner brags in the open:
snorting, he walks puffed up,
the sun showers him
with the last rays of gold
as he carries the crown
of another grazing day.

Kitaku

When I first saw it,
it was young and healthy:
children snapped fingers
it barked and bounced
with delight

Days rolled on:
it attained maturity
- a strong, white dog
with small patches
of sharply defined black
over the head and tail

Flames of ill luck
leaked its way:
it suffered severe neglect,
to quieten pangs of hunger,
it turned to faeces,
skins and even rotten eggs
from scattered homes

It attained such cleverness,
stalking into some hut,
like a ghost,
it would walk off
with bowls of hidden meals

Moved to boiling anger,
the youth of the village
assembled in an afternoon;
armed to teeth
with clubs and matchets,
they hunted the beast
a cloud of dust rising
with solid intent,
of immediate death

It got wind of danger:
sharp and slippery,
it vanished out of sight;
trapped in a hut,
a mob brandished weapons
and swore with excitement;
like a slippery fish
it slid between legs
disappearing like a flea

Time wound up,
pain, terror and solitude
converged from all sides:
dog-fights at festivities
ended with wounding defeat
of him,
always crushed to bare earth

He absorbed such lots,
at long last
even cruel death
was moved to pity:
this limping infirmity
disappeared
into thick, thorny thickets
where an intoxicating stench
betrayed its last remains.

Mee! Mee, Meeee!..........

High ebbs of tension
of an uplifted head,
visibly unable to graze:
Meee! Mee, Meeee!.......

On the way home,
she leads the way
bleating unceasingly:
Mee! Meee!...........

On reaching her shed,
she becomes intoxicated
with waves restlessness
smelling from lamb to lamb
but in vain:
Meee! Meee!.............

It is a touching death-stroke
on a week-old lamb
which so weepingly
maternal cheeks wets:
Meee! Mee, Meee!..............

The Spring that Flows

A spring flows
from the foot
of our hill;
when rains fall,
canals, rivers
redden with
brown earth, but
our spring
is ever clear

Murmuring against
mute, slippery stones,
it crawls out
gently and windingly;
its banks evergreen,
long reeds flap
cheers of escort
to distant arid plains

The spring teems with
frightful crabs,
horned fish,
green snakes
and a python
delights sunning and wriggling
along the marshy banks

Older than the village,
the ancestors drank
from its eyes:
tales of its past
emerge linking
the present
with the past

The spring that flows
from the foot of our hill
will ever flow on
while competing with time,
our children
will drink from it,
feed from the salad
which enriches their blood

Saturday Comes

Saturday comes,
down and up hills,
neck-bending loads
of maize, millet, bananas,
clay-pots and squeaking chicken
stream to the market place

By a busy roadside,
commotion of bargains
pervade the touches
of exciting business;
a tethered donkey brays
heightening the intensity
of a lively day
as a drunkard sways off
urinating zig-zags
along a path
spitting out insults
like a charging cobra

At a corner, far away
cries of thief! Thief!........
Relay across:
a slight fellow in tartters
is pulled to the ground;
in no time, kicks, clubs
and stones rain on him;
like frightened mice,
the mob leaves him dying

Across the Western hills,
the sun turns blood-red;
the great day ages,
paths fill up
with pounding paces
as women returning home
prate about the exciting day.

Our Day

When the next brew
was ready,
we saw him again:
the joke-cracker
always sparked to his best
by waves of alcohol

Our day pregnant,
we gathered around
our breasts calm,
our faces sober

He mounted the occasion:
our jaws flew   ajar
as spurts of laughter
warmed up the air

Even though he sauntered off
tearing himself away
and stubbornly resisting
our pressing pleas,
our day shone bright
like full moon.

Celebrated Marriage

The week before,
Mangusha also married;
the whole village
was filled with the event

Relatives contributed
happily and heavily;
various duties found
quick willingness

A big bull
fell to the occasion:
overfilled with food,
stomachs bulged out

The dance
following the highlights
of the great day
was gruel-thick:
many retired to bed
with aches of tiredness

The local brewer
had done his best
men conversed in gaiety,
their tones elevated;
a voice took delight
teasing the unmarried lot:
"Marry in daylight
like Mangusha!
Put an end
to nightly stealing"

Intoxicated
with jubilation,
old women added on
in echoes of ululations:
"No old one misses
a mother in law!"

When Kimalo Goes Hunting

When Kimalo goes hunting,
Au! au, au!...............

His dogs
starved for a day,
they will comb hills,
and swampy rivers,
au! au! au!.................

A hare will spring up,
up and down,
zig, zag and
straight on
driven by currents
of deadly fear,
au! au! au!................

Simba, the bravest
will sharply dive
on its delicate neck,
au! au! au!.................

Amidst protests
of shrieks and kicks ,
he will crunch
its neck with pride,
au! au! au!................

The delighted master
will quicken his paces
to the exciting scene,
he will hack the hare
to tasty portions
for his dogs
au! au! au!................

The dogs will storm bushes
with renewed fierceness,
birds will fly high
to tree-tops,
squirrels
will scamper
off to deep crevices:
the hunting day
will unfold with bright promises
aù! au! au!..................

Tax - Collection

The headman on the lead,
hurly burly,
men follow behind

At a home,
they suddenly stop
enquire from puzzled faces
the whereabouts of a father

In no time,
a sling flies round
a ram's neck;
fat and big ,
the animal is led away
bleating along the paths

The children,
who in harmony had played
freeze with fear,
others shed tears,
all so incomprehensible!

But the headman presses on
a chain of men behind,
amidst protesting shouts,
they threaten to seize everything:
the village is shaken to its foundations

Across an open ground,
they lead a smooth calf,
two goats and a bleating ram;
behind follow heaps
of maize, beans, coffee
all to be auctioned soon

A stranger stares on dazzled
but many people know:
it is season again
for the headman
to be on the move
collecting taxes
without mercy.

The Village Path

The overhead sun bright,
the air fresh and light,
one paces along twists
and curves of an ancient path
along which bananas-stalks stand
like soldiers at attention

The earth dark and rich,
a file of shiny, red ants
hurriedly crosses the path
in reverse directions
celebrating fine touches
of escaping vapour while a mole,
betrayed by light
moves stupified aimlessly

Along a winding bend,
an old bananas-stalk droops
in insupportable age,
ripe bananas smear the air
with currents of sweet air
which sets mouths watering

Across a wooden bridge
a stream gurgles down,
the path suddenly bursts
into an open ground
and leads on into a cow-path,
devastated by hooves:
on and on it drags on
fading into the distant horizon.

When the Monkey Comes Again

When the monkey comes again
to feast on green maize,
an army of us will be there
to deliver a lesson unforgettable
before escaping to tree-tops

Ears triggered,
hair ruffled up
tails straight with speed,
our thin village-dogs
will fiercely chase
as stones and clubs
whirr through the air:
Huyooo! kamata.............
Huyooo! kamata.............

Upon arresting one,
we shall club it to death,
slaughter it there as
a feast for the dogs;
our spears ornamented
with bits of monkey-skin,
we shall return home
success tickling
our adventurous hearts

Our dogs ,more fierce,
thieves,wild beasts
and even neighbours
will timely be checked:
our farms will yield
heavy harvests and
hunger,a constant threat
will be held at a distance.

The Wind that Came

The wind that came
started from the East
our clothes fluttered
about us
as we traversed the plains

Scurrying over fields,
spinning magic whirled up,
a cloud of dust
like a thick smoke rose up:
the sky became a turmoil
of flying shapes

Swishing and fluffing,
trees heaved up and down,
rhythm pervaded the air
the world in a grip of frenzy,
heavy boughs like rags
were torn off tree-trunks

The sun weak like a dying beast,
fear mounted within
as we tightly gripped
thickets and trees
calling on our mothers
for help

The wind cast
its heaviest anger
through the village:
estates of banana-stalks
were flattened like grass,
a hut of a friend crumbled down
and lay like a dead cow

A mother in pitiful wrinkles
meant that severe hunger
was at door-entrances
but an old man insisted stubbornly
that the devil had just passed.

On the Path when Dark

Pitch dark,
a worried mother
plodded through the plains
hurriedly as her breathless child
ran beside her
loads crushing their spines

Above the heads
maize-stalks locked arms:
the air tense,
hearts crumbled with fear
when bats fluttered
and squeaked in thickets

Those vivid tales
of lions, recently seen,
of poisonous snakes, killed,
of a man gorged to death
by a charging buffalo and
of throat-cutters
who sucked people dry
attained renewed vigour

Their necks stiff
with pains,
clothes wet from sweat,
the Northern star
flickered protection
all along;
they reached home
where a worried man
was on the verge of departure
to look for them

A night meal cooked fast
the dreams that followed
were horrors of lions,
serpents and throat-cutters
which set the child frightfully screaming
and sweating from all pores.

Crying all the Time

On a dusty ground,
a lump of helplessness
on delicate little legs
tries to stand in vain:
flapping stumpy wings,
crying all the time

Bulging eyes
breaking through
skinny eyelids
and a fine beak
taking shape,
it struggles,
falls down many times,
crying all the time

Above the earth,
stretches a branch
upon which a loose
old nest hangs;
its bottom gaping,
the wind takes pleasure
threatening to blow it off

Chuckling furiously,
a mother emerges suddenly:
she flies about
calling her dear one;
she dives with iron-courage
scooping off her little one
into the hanging nest

From various directions
of the vast wilderness,
she collects reeds
repairing her house

with burning concern
as the little one
moves about restlessly,
jaws wide apart,
expecting food
crying all the time.

The Strength of Soup

The butcher's knife
worked on a fat bull:
the meat hanging
needs no advertizing

Unable to resist
such an offer,
a mother unearths
all her savings
over several seasons:
she warms up the path
to bargain for a big cut

Flashing her eyes,
the meat is so inviting,
she settles for a fat hunk
most ideal for soup;
rolling it in a lump,
she retires home
confident and proud

She mounts her best pot,
bright flames cheer it up
as it steams with meat
the smell inviting;
even dogs in her neighbourhood
bark apprehensively

The pot alighted,
she sits on her lawn
sipping hot soup,
chunks of meat going round:
children belch satiated,
sweat trickles down the brows

The overhead moon bright,
blood rises to brinks,
though life is mean,
there will always be days
when the strength of soup
will lift up petty life
close to full moon.

Ooo Nkanroko, Oyaiyoo.......

When thatching an old roof
or weeding a field,
the intensity
of an unaging song
bursts forth from
industrious village-women:
Ooo Nkanroko, Oyaiyoo!..........

Her hut always filthy
teeming with bugs, fleas
and fat rats,
her roof leaking
like a tree
with a thin canopy,
Oyaiyoo!

Her firewood wet,
her cooking slow
and the very meals
untasty and unworthy
of a young wife,
Oyaiyooo!

Her fields idle bushes
or the very last
to be broken,
her promising crop
always strangled
by tall weeds,
and when she tightens,
her arms for a day's labour
her hoe is a dangling stump!
Ooo Nkanroko, Oyaiyoo!........

Along the paths,
she weaves and spreads
poisonous gossip
like hungry flames and
sets neighbours
against one another,
Oyaiyoo!

Her husband's herds,
once uncountable and healthy,
now a few skeletons
peeling away watery eyes,
oyaiyoo!

Ooo Nkanroko, Oyaiyoo........
the reddenning sun
far in the Western arm
disappears behind trees,
small flies hum over heads,
the day's labour done,
night descends slowly
each retiring home!

Bitterness in Darkness

At night,
when everybody was home,
accusations flared up,
often pinning him down
the black sheep
in the family

Tormented by a disgusting life,
his delicate heart
unravelled unending details
which he alone
pondered into depths
of uncountable nights;
had he not withstood
such heaps as would have
wetted several maternal cheeks?

The turmoil of worries
boiled down to a constant
frame of mind:
he quietly disappeared
into solitudes of darkness
there, he would bear agony
among squeaking bats
and howling, nightly beasts

Although cast away,
the dark blanket above
allowed distant, sympathetic eyes
to cheer up the world.

The Witch, Oho! the Witch

When pitch dark,
well past midnight,
she moves about
doing her lot

The village wakes up
death smeared
on door-entrances:
woes sink a new day

Elders assemble:
amidst wrangles
of fierce discussions,
a resolution is filtered:
a curse is spelt

Ancestors stir
in their graves,
a trembling, old woman
vows pleadingly
not to have harmed
any mother's child:
the spirit-world frowns,
days of the witch contract

The witch,
Oho!
The witch!

Brought to the eyes
of the villagers,
spears clatter!
Warm blood flows!
Hearts bathe
in felt vengeance!

The Peel of full Moon

The peel of full moon
excites the village;
full of merriment,
children delight
in plays and songs,
echoes of laughter
mingle with night air

From above,
the heavenly ball
reflects mystical strength:
old minds unwind
fascinating stories
and minds stray off
to strange lands
of thrilling adventures

As if gone mad,
an old dog finds pleasure
barking at the moon;
bush-babies set on
relays of vibrant screams:
a straying wind
sweeps across soothingly
and life vibrates
in various felt tunes.

Suspicion

After the sun is tired,
sooty darkness
hangs over the village:
no roads,
only twisting paths,
no lights
only glowing worms

On the way home,
bats squeak
in frightful relays,
banana-leaves rustle
and suspicion like flames
burns high:
an animal on attack,
or a thief on the run?

The village has a dog
as fierce as a lion:
once it lost its head:
it attacked a boy on errand
inflicting such gashes,
he was reduced to a cripple

The village harbours a mad man
who roams about aimlessly:
he smashed a neighbor's pot
to pieces and strangled
a sheep to death;
when in a wild state:
he sets forth
currents of fear
to both children and women

Kilala we, Kilala we...........

Elected headman,
his bonny form
filled up,
he wore round cheeks,
a protruding belly,
and a soggy behind

His dusty name
was elevated
with riches,
his giggles and
frequent laughters
above banana-thickness,
his little head
fell victim of pomposity:
he ruled with appetites
callously trampling
on other people

A wind blew:
he was deflated
to bare earth:
he became a snail
creeping back
to its shell

Those soft curves,
the commanding tone
he had acquired,
his vociferous fame
all blown off
like fog;
embraced by disappointment
in a pool of loneliness,
he fell back
and sighed:
"Illusion! Myth!"

Only that the local musicians
timely got grip of it:
the replays of a song
rise with shattering intensity:
"Kilala.. we, Kilala... we,
Uu mubayaa............"

Devil on Walk

The silence
of night reigning,
immersed in dreams,
the village snores

Along a village-path,
pounding trots begin:
a sharp, squeaky voice
pierces the darkness:
wailing and cursing,
with bewildering strangeness

The thickness
of banana-growth
replays the loudness,
fear paralyzes hearts;
one crouches double,
eyes tightly closed
against the devil
as he ventures again
into mysterious trots

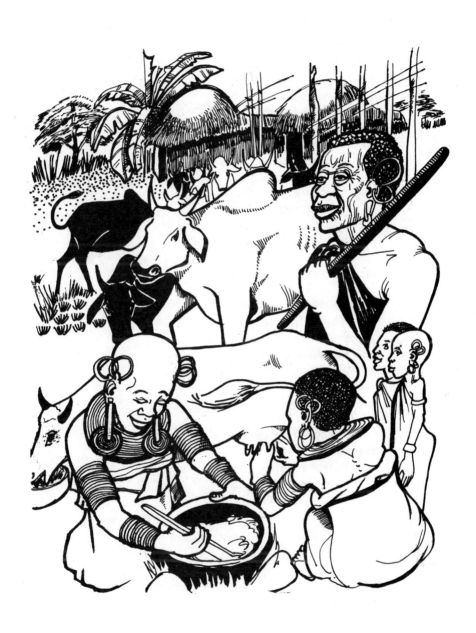

Home Coming of a Cattle-Her

The bright day over,
an evening ripened slowly:
wings fluttered here and there,
from clustering bushes,
squeaks pierced frightfully,
chicken settled gently
in their nightly shack

At a kraal-entrance,
an old man took sentry,
eyes flickering curiously,
he delightfully absorbed
the home coming of a herd

On nearing home,
the cows quickened paces
mooing all along;
the calves in the cattle-sheds
kicked about in frenzy
as their hunger heightened,
their mouths watering

A mother, who busily
had been cooking,
suspended all else:
summoning her daughter,
their fingers worked
on soft, warm udders
their wide-mouthed gourds
warmed up with milk

The wide, dark sky
blinked and winked
with competing dots
of distant flames:
the old man retired
to his sooty chamber;
after a hot meal
a quiet night stalked in.

Witchcraft

Streaks of grey hair peeping
from a dark forest,
mysterious life has enviously chosen
to drown a neighbour
with mounting problems

She has bravely fought
through corrugations
of an exacting life;
her patience deep,
she had been tranquil
in a stormy sea

But strangely,
unexpected currents
have come to peaks:
she walks alone
murmuring and talking
endlessly;
avoiding company
like an island,
she is spurts of laughter
and spontaneous tears
all in one

Her closest friends
vividly recall her best days
when she had stood firmly
in difficult knots of life;
looking at her now,
they curse the witch
believing beyond doubts,
malevolence was driving her
without direction.

You, who Dared

You, who
in dark concealment
into my farm dared,
you, who reaped the fattest of my crop,
disclose yourself
before time runs out!

You will see!
Your belly will go up
like that of croaking toad,
you will vomit till
your lungs and intestines
get stuck upon your throat,
upon this,
a cock will crow
in your bowels,
grinding pains will eat you up
till you willingly
go on your knees
at my door-entrance,
crying for forgiveness!

You may despise my word,
you may play clever,
I tell you,
your head will go nuts:
you will talk alone,
laugh and cry
along the ways,
you will walk naked
like a beast!
You will even eat your faeces!

You, who
into my farm dared,
tremors will betray you.

the look of your eyes
will betray you,
your ancestry-chain
will come to a dead end
like that of a mule!

Come out soon,
lest devils begin
to assail you,
this is your last chance
before the door
shuts permanently!

Who Crosses my Fertility-Chain

What eats away my children,
I daughter of fertile ancestors?
Who robs me of maternal pride,
when babies are in my embraces?

The stomach of one swelled up,
his eyes sank in,
his chest bellowed;
after few nights,
life was gone out of him

A beckoning adventure
on a tree-top
suddenly stopped
the life of another:
mercilessly disfigured,
he was a lump
of broken bones, oozing
blood from all sides

The third,
the healthiest,
a sweet girl of enviable
charms and virtues:
caught in the midst
of a stormy river,
she was swept away
like a lost reed

The last one,
my only hope,
shared a mother's cooking,
ever since then;
stomach pains
have taken root:
her life hangs in the air,

a violent wind
to sweep it
where it wills:

What curse do I bear?
Who crosses my fertility-chain,
I daughter of a full mother,
a sister in the house of plenty:
Which rituals must I undergo
to appease the world of ancestry?

My Violent Stick

The day hot and dreary,
a long stick in hand,
I came to a silent pool
of lush green
as I wandered about

Driven by throbbing curiosity,
I raised my stick high
violently ripping off
a wide opening

At the base,
I discovered a dirty,
old nest in which,
tiny, blind mice
screamed helplessly
as a frantic mother
dashed off with fear

In simmering heat
the bush stood still
weeping round, milky tears
which moistened
the dusty earth

The many times
I had cut fingers
or stumbled and bled
settled on my mind;
as if accused,
I stood still
staring at the tip tap
dripping to mother earth.